CHOICES FOR GRADUATES

*True Stories of Young People,
and the Decisions
that Determined Their Destinies*

Al Janssen

BAKER BOOK HOUSE
Grand Rapids, Michigan 49516

ISBN: 0-8010-5225-4

The King James Version is the primary Scripture source in this book.
Other translations used are the New International Version (NIV) and
The Living Bible (TLB).

Printed in the United States of America

Contents

Prologue:
Choose This Day

The great warrior-chieftain was dying. During his 110 years, he'd risen from the rank of a humble slave to chief-of-state of a great nation. Under his leadership an army had conquered pagan tribes and consolidated the land. Finally, after many years of conflict, the country was at peace.

Now there would be a change in leadership. Couriers hurried to deliver the message to all the tribes. Elders, chiefs, judges, and tribal officials were summoned to a great assembly. After a time of worship, the great general stood to address the crowd. A cheer went up as they saw their leader, but he raised his arm, asking for silence. Instantly a hush fell over the men, as they leaned forward to catch his every word.

Softly, with just a hint of a crack in his aging voice, he began to review the historical events that had forged this unique nation. It had all started with one man, called by God to leave his home and idols and come to a new land that God would give him. His sons had settled in this country until famine forced them to move to Egypt. There they grew into a mighty people, more than 2 million strong, but they were oppressed. Until God miraculously rescued them out of slavery and brought them back to this land he had chosen for them.

The leader's voice was strong and confident. He reminded his people that God had given them this land, with cities they did not build and vineyards and olive groves they did not plant. "Now fear the Lord," the chief announced. "Throw away the gods your forefathers worshiped, and serve the Lord."

As though he was gathering all of his strength for this final exhortation, he shouted, "*Choose for yourselves this day whom you will serve,* whether the gods your forefathers served beyond the river, or the gods of the Amorites, in whose land you are living. *But as for me and my household, we will serve the Lord!*"

It was an electric moment. As one, the crowd roared in response: "Far be it from us to forsake the Lord and serve other gods!"

Certainly this remains one of the high points in Israel's history. The great leader who issued this challenge was Joshua. And in this incident, we see the secret of his success.

It would be easy to review Joshua's career and focus on his achievements. Out of twelve spies, he was one of only two who believed they could go in and conquer the land. When the majority ruled, Joshua had to spend forty years wandering in the wilderness with his countrymen. After the death of Moses, Joshua was given the mantle of leadership. He oversaw the great triumph at Jericho when the walls came tumbling down. He guided the Israelites to many victories over the pagan people of that land.

But the secret of Joshua's life was not in his achievements. It was in his decisions.

Early in his life, Joshua chose to follow God. He often stayed at the tent of meeting, after Moses had left, just to be near the Lord. He chose to obey God's laws, and to meditate on his words. That was why he prospered; that was why he was successful.

It's the same today.

Choices. We face them today. They can be as simple as deciding which TV show to watch or what brand of soft drink to buy or which friend to visit. They can hold long-term implications: Which college do I attend? What career should I pursue? Should I marry now or wait?

The latter decisions have lifelong ramifications. We usually make them only after a great deal of thought. But there are other choices, equally important. Often, we don't stop to think about them; we simply respond. We may not even realize that we've made a choice—but we have.

What kind of decisions?

Choices about God: Do I believe him and give my life to him? Or do I chase after the idols of career, money, popularity, or self-indulgence?

Choices about ethics: Do I follow the laws and principles of Scripture? Or do I determine my own standards for right and wrong?

Choices about coping with disappointment and tragedy: Do I trust that God has a plan? Or do I try and make sense of it myself?

These decisions affect whom we marry and our attitudes about family. They govern our career moves. They influence our methods of problem solving. They impact how we relate to our peers and those in authority over us.

This short book is about choices/decisions. It's a series of stories about men and women like you. Each of them faced choices:

To yield to political pressure or heed conscience

To repay a debt or declare bankruptcy

To give up after failure or press on with a vocation

To fulfill sexual fantasy or control lusts

To strive for personal glory or the glory of God.

The decisions these people made had consequences—for good and for ill. And so it is with us. We all must make choices. Even choosing not to choose is a choice. And *all* of our choices will have consequences.

This book does not attempt to preach or tell you what direction you should go. You must make those decisions yourself. But perhaps these stories will inspire you—or warn you—or cause you to take a little more time to think ahead—to count the cost to . . .

. . . choose whom you will serve.

Let's begin, then, with a story about a man who faced a choice that could cut short his career. Should he obey the President of the United States? Or follow his conscience?

To Fear God or Man

1

If you're in politics, you play by the rules. I help you, you help me. Occasionally, you have to compromise. That's normal. That's how the system works.

But where does conviction enter the picture? When does a person stand on principle and refuse to play the political game anymore? Regardless of the cost. Even if it means the end of his career?

George Reed had reason to be concerned. The man addressing him was the Attorney General of the United States, John Mitchell. A few years earlier, Mitchell had phoned Reed on behalf of the President of the United States, Richard Nixon, and offered him the job as Chairman of the United States Parole Board. Now, the Attorney General was asking—no, demanding—a favor.

The situation was simple. There was a certain prisoner that the President wanted released. His parole hearing was scheduled in a couple of weeks. This man had access to significant amounts of money and would sway many votes. His release could virtually guarantee Nixon's reelection to a second term.

Already, two key men in the Justice Department had put pressure on Reed. To each he patiently explained, "I cannot permit the Parole Board's decision to be influenced by any political considerations." Besides, Reed added, he was only one vote on the board.

Next the Attorney General tried his hand. "Your board will follow your lead," Mitchell said. "They respect your judgment." Reed was also reminded that Mitchell would support Reed's reappointment as Parole Chairman after the election. In addition, Mitchell promised action on a much-needed increase in budget and new parole legislation that Reed had advocated for some time.

The message was clear. Play the game right, and he was guaranteed six more years in office—plus the resources to do the job the way he believed it should be done.

Refuse, and he would be looking for a job. Not only that, a long-standing friendship with Mitchell would be broken.

What should he do? Were Mitchell and the President really asking too much? Until now, they had kept their promise to never try to influence Parole Board decisions. Was it right that they ask this one small favor in return?

Reed thought back to a critical moment in his life and career more than twenty years before.

At that time, he was head of Prevention and Parole Services for the Minnesota Youth Conservation Commission. It was a cabinet-level position for the Governor of Minnesota. And heady responsibility for a young man. In fact, the Governor was so impressed that he often sent Reed to fill many of his speaking engagements.

The Governor and Reed also shared a common Christian faith. They spoke openly about their love for Christ. Together they persuaded the legislature to adopt a bold, comprehensive program to help youthful offenders exit the prison system ready to function in society.

Then they ran into problems. A teenager committed suicide at the state reformatory. Next it was discovered that a few years before, guards had killed some prisoners and buried them in the reformatory yard. Of course, that had happened long before Reed came to Minnesota. Nevertheless, the press and the Governor's political enemies demanded an investigation. And the new programs the Governor and Reed had planned to push through the legislature looked doomed.

It was a frustrating time for George. One morning, as he was driving to work, he felt overwhelmed by the circumstances. He couldn't face the uproar at the office. As he passed the airport, he pulled off the highway and began to sob. Up until that point, George Reed had felt there was nothing he couldn't handle. Now, all of his programs, hopes, and dreams were on the brink of dying.

Reed poured out his heart to God. He admitted his proud, self-centered ways. He begged God for the comfort of his Holy Spirit. In return, he promised to serve God in any way he might lead.

Finally, he heard a still, small voice say, "Why don't you let me take full charge of your life?"

That seemed so logical. Immediately, he answered, "Yes, Lord, I surrender George Reed and his future to you."

At that point, he made a commitment. He would do his work in a way that was pleasing to God, regardless of what anybody else thought. No doubt, there would be times when that conflicted with the current political climate. *But he would fear God instead of man.*

A few days later, the investigation was completed. It showed no wrongdoing on Reed's part. And the legislature granted all the necessary finances to expand the program. The Governor had won a major victory.

That was a dramatic moment. From that point on, Reed's relationship with God was the primary driving force in his life. He wasn't even surprised when he received a call from Washington, D.C. Would he be willing to serve on the U.S. Parole Board? And help launch a Federal Youth Correction Program? And would he meet with the President?

As the awesomeness of that moment hit him, God

reminded him, to "Fear no man!" God was in control of his life. He had opened up this opportunity for service.

So Reed served the country under President Eisenhower, who eventually appointed him as Chairman of the Parole Board. He continued to serve under Presidents Kennedy and Johnson.

The job of the eight-member federal parole board is to review the cases of thousands of inmates in the federal prison system. It's a huge responsibility. These men and women determine how much time each convict must serve of his sentence beyond the mandated minimum. They determine if a convict is safe to return to society, or if the danger is such that he must be kept locked up for the protection of the majority.

As chairman of the board, Reed wielded great influence. When political pressure was exerted, he felt the brunt of it. He'd received thousands of letters urging him to release the infamous Bird Man of Alcatraz. He'd confronted such notorious criminals as Alger Hiss and Charles Manson.

But inevitably, there came a major test of his loyalty. Would he fulfill his legally mandated responsibilities as unto the Lord, or bow to powerful human pressure?

During a routine hearing, he faced a labor racketeer. As Reed reviewed the case, he learned about the man's business dealings with the Mafia and was convinced that his release was not in the public interest.

President Johnson wasn't pleased with the decision. He wanted the prisoner paroled immediately. After all, this man had headed up a union fund-raising drive for his reelection campaign. And Reed's term expired in eight months.

Reed referred the decision to the entire parole board. A six-to-two vote sustained his original order, denying parole, at which point, he learned the President would not recommend his reappointment. Reed then taught college until Mitchell invited him back to his old post.

Now Reed faced a similar, though potentially more explosive dilemma. Before accepting Mitchell's invitation, he had insisted that the President agree that parole board decisions would be free from all political pressures. The President and Attorney General Mitchell had kept that agreement. Until now. This one time— it was important, for the nation, they said.

Was he willing to risk President Nixon's reelection on principle? Was this one prisoner really so dangerous to the American people that he couldn't be released now? Reed really didn't want to pack up his belongings, find a new job, and move again. How he wished he could just walk away from this emotionally charged situation.

But he couldn't. He'd made the decision many years ago to do what he believed was right—even if it might cost him his career. He would not compromise. The facts of the case, not politics, would dictate his and the board's actions.

And the facts were overwhelming. When Mitchell demanded an answer, Reed calmly suggested, "If you and the President would review the file, you would also vote to deny parole."

It was obvious by Mitchell's expression that their friendship was over. Reed no longer had the support of the President. But he knew he was right.

And just who was this prisoner who attracted the attention of the nation's highest office? A man by the name of Jimmy Hoffa, president of the International Brotherhood of Teamsters, the nation's largest and most powerful labor union.

Hoffa was in prison for jury tampering and for mail and wire fraud. There were other even more serious charges: evidence concerning misappropriation of pension funds; skimming of profits from pension fund investments; *and* extensive ties with organized crime—the Mafia.

There was no question that this man could influence a presidential campaign. An endorsement from the Teamsters meant many votes. And a large contribution to Nixon's campaign was promised, *if*. . . . Simply put, Hoffa's release would virtually guarantee Nixon's election.

The parole board's job was to judge whether it was safe to society if this man was released. And on that score, the facts were overwhelming.

Reed knew he had to do what his conscience dictated was right. So he would trust God to take care of the outcome.

The board denied Hoffa parole.

But that is not the end of the story.

Four months later, President Nixon signed an executive grant of clemency for Hoffa, commuting his sentence from thirteen years to six-and-a-half. That made Hoffa eligible for immediate release.

The next year, Nixon was reelected in a landslide.

But then came Watergate. Nixon resigned in disgrace.

John Mitchell was one of several Nixon aides who went to prison in the aftermath of the scandal.

And when Mitchell's turn for a parole hearing came up, guess whom he had to face? George Reed, who'd been reappointed as Chairman of the Parole Board by President Ford.

And Jimmy Hoffa? He disappeared in 1975. To this day, no one knows what happened to him, but most believe he was victimized by his former partners in crime.

So George Reed did what he thought was right. He followed God, not man.

And God had the last word.[1]

Learning from Failure 2

It was a dark and stormy night.

In "Peanuts," Snoopy gets laughs for typing that line, while seated on top of his doghouse. It's considered the penultimate opening sentence for a novel. No one would think to use it today. It's too corny. Not creative.

So you might be surprised to learn that there's a very popular children's novel that opens with that statement. It's an innovative story that has excited and encouraged readers for years. In fact, it won the Newberry Award, the highest honor for children's writing.

And it almost wasn't printed.

When you look at this author today, you see tremendous success—more than twenty-five books published, many prestigious awards, respected teacher of writing. But behind her *Who's Who* listing is another picture. There are at least six more book manuscripts that lie in her home—unpublished. And there was a string of some ten years during which she wrote and saw virtually no publishing success.

"If I'm not free to fail, I'm not free to take risks," she says, "and everything in life that's worth doing involves a willingness to take a risk and involves the risk of failure."

Often we don't see this side of success. We forget that the major league baseball player once toiled in the minors. The company president probably started his climb in the warehouse or the mail room. And during their climb to the top, there were setbacks. No doubt, there were days when they wondered whether the effort was worthwhile.

The author we're talking about wrote her first story at the age of five. She wrote because she was an only child who loved books. When she'd read all the stories in her bookcase, the only way she could get more was to write them herself.

In the process of writing, she was also able to sort through some of the confusions of life. In her created world, it didn't matter that she was slightly lame or unpopular at school. It didn't hurt so much that her parents gave her little attention. She didn't care that her teachers thought she was stupid.

She was anything but dumb. Out of her fertile imagination came many short stories and poems. From libraries she borrowed books and read voraciously. And in stories, hers and others, she began to understand the meaning of life.

By the time she entered college, she knew she wanted to be a writer. Of course, that meant being published. And there was some early success with the publication of several novels.

Failure might have been easier to accept if there hadn't been that initial success. But the taste of publication only fueled the desire for more. A painter wants people to view his paintings. A composer desires that her music be performed. And a writer needs to have her books read.

But this writer went into an extended slump. They were tough years in many respects. She was married. She had two children. The family moved out of New York City into a Connecticut country village. There they ran a general store. It was a tough way to earn a living. They were on a financial precipice. Their two-hundred-year-old farm house could not be kept warm in the winter. It was hard to find acceptance in the tightly-knit Yankee community.

And her manuscripts were rejected. She continued to write. But virtually everything she submitted for publication was returned. Clipped to those dreaded rejection slips:

> Thank you for giving us the opportunity to review your manuscript. However, after careful evaluation,

our editors have concluded that it would not fit in with
our current publishing plans. . . .

Year after year, it continued. She wondered if she
should give up—call it a career—stick to family responsibilities and the country store.

It came to a head over a novel that had made the
rounds of several publishing houses. It had spent several weeks at one house, and the editors were divided.
They wanted another opinion. The verdict reached her
on her fortieth birthday.

Rejection!

This seemed like an obvious sign to stop writing.
For too long she had plunged her energies into this
profession. Her children complained that she couldn't
make a decent pie crust. Whites and colors too frequently got mixed in the washing. She felt guilty,
thinking she wasn't being a good wife and mother. It
was time to put her dreams behind her and get on
with the job at hand.

Solemnly she stood in her study and draped the
cover over her typewriter. The tears couldn't be contained. She felt miserable.

Yet in the midst of that moment, her mind started
conjuring up the plot for a novel about failure. She
stopped, sat down and recorded her feelings in her
journal. She writes that it was a:

> moment of decision. . . . I had to write. I had no choice
> in the matter. It was not up to me to say I would stop,
> because I could not. It didn't matter how small or in-

adequate my talent. If I never had another book published, and it was very clear to me that this was a real possibility, I still had to go on writing.

During this period she was also questioning the faith of her youth. She read theology books and found them unsatisfying. Many of the dogmas of the church seemed restrictive. Four of her closest friends had died within two years. She wanted to know what happens to people when they die. She wanted to know why, if God is so loving and good, do the wicked flourish and the innocent suffer? Was he a punitive, angry God, out to get us? Or a God who loves us unequivocally?

She wrestled with those issues in the local country church, with a group of high school students. She was their teacher, but she didn't use any curriculum. The kids had enough materials in school. Instead they talked about the world, and their lives, and how the two fit within a universe created by a loving God.

The teenagers asked questions—big questions, like the ones she was asking. One question led to another. There seemed to be more questions than answers. They found some answers in the Bible. Others came from unexpected sources.

One was a book by the great scientist Albert Einstein. He wrote that anyone who is not lost in rapturous awe at the power and glory of the mind behind the universe is as good as a burnt-out candle. What a strange place to find theology!

Our author began reading books about post-

Newtonian science. Quantum theory and relativity. A story started flowing out of her study—a story that merged science and theology. It involved a little girl who felt ugly and unloved and misunderstood, and how she faced a situation that required incredible courage.

It was science fantasy, written for children. It traveled into new, faraway worlds. It opened up the wonder and mystery of great scientific discoveries. It dealt with the ageless battle between the powers of light and darkness. It stretched the mind and lifted the spirit.

Most of all, it demonstrated the power of love. *And how love wins!*

As the book developed, some of those perplexing theological issues gained perspective. She realized she could never plumb the depths of God—no more than she could understand all the discoveries of science and the wonders of the universe. But she *could* recognize God's love. And she could affirm the power of that love which created this universe.

As she wrote, she began to realize that her writing was not just a career. It was a vocation—a calling from God. This story was emerging out of her love for God. It was attempting to reveal his light and love in a fresh way. When she was finished, she knew it was the best writing she'd ever done.

It was also different. That scared the publishers. They read the manuscript and appreciated the quality of writing. But it was too difficult for children, they said. Adults would have trouble understanding it. It needed to be changed. Cut. Rearranged.

She disagreed. It was a book for children. Only children *could* understand it. She would not change it.

For the next two-and-a-half years, more than thirty publishers turned it down. "It's so ironic," she wrote in her journal, "that I wrote this book for God, and I wrote this book because I finally understand why I'm a writer, and now nobody wants me."

She finally gave up hope that the book would be published; yet she was willing to accept herself as a writer, whether she was published or not. It was her calling. She *had* to write.

Let's be thankful that a publisher finally saw the light. Farrar, Straus & Giroux agreed to take her book, even though they didn't then publish juvenile books. It deserved to be in print, they said. However, they warned her that it wouldn't sell very many copies.

Thankfully, publishers aren't omniscient. That book—*A Wrinkle in Time*—has become a classic. It's sold millions of copies, and touched children and adults everywhere. She has gone on to write many other wonderful books, like *The Young Unicorns*, *A Wind in the Door*, and *A Swiftly Tilting Planet*.

The author, Madeleine L'Engle, is humbled by her success. "Quite a few people have come to me and said that they have become Christians because of my books," she says.

It's appropriate that Madeleine have the last word in this story—from her books *Walking on Water* and *A Circle of Quiet:*

I have to try, but I do not have to succeed. Following Christ has nothing to do with success as the world sees success. It has to do with love.

During the ten years when practically nothing I wrote was published, I was as much writer qua writer as I am now; it may happen that there will come another time when I can't find anyone to publish my work. If this happens, it will matter. It will hurt. But I did learn, on that fortieth birthday, that success is not my motivation.

I am grateful for that terrible birthday, which helps me to wear glass slippers lightly, very lightly.[2]

A Modern Philosopher 3

How much impact can one man have on society? As we're about to see, a lot more than you might expect. One man, with a keen sense of timing, insight into his culture and people's desires, plus a little luck, can actually change the thinking of an entire generation.

The person we're about to meet is not a politician or entertainer. He's not a famous athlete or media star. Yet his influence is evident in our advertising, music, mass media, and lifestyles. In fact, you might say he has come to symbolize a whole way of thinking.

We really can't say that this individual invented something or expressed any new, profound thoughts. He only exposed and "made respectable" something that people already desired.

29

He is a lithe, almost sickly-looking person. He lives amidst the trappings of phenomenal wealth, ensconced in a mansion on five acres of Holmby Hills. That's a small southern California community wedged between Bel Air and Beverly Hills. He rarely leaves the grounds, preferring instead to indulge in all the luxuries of life that he's bought and stored on his estate.

A staff of ninety servants execute his every whim. A chef is constantly on call. A team of technicians fill video tapes with specified television programs, minus commercials, for viewing at his convenience. There are butlers, gardeners, maintenance men, and housekeepers. One full-time employee spends her every working day filling volume after volume of scrapbooks with articles and mementos of her employer. Several hundred volumes document his influence on society.

To anyone who likes to get out and do things, the lifestyle of this man is surprisingly bland. He sleeps until three or four in the afternoon. Sometimes he doesn't even bother to get dressed, conducting business meetings in his pajamas. These meetings begin around 5:00 in the afternoon when the offices of the rest of his empire—HMH Enterprises—are closing for the day.

Once his business is concluded, it's playtime. Three nights a week he plays Monopoly with old friends. Two other nights he throws a party. The format is always the same—guests enjoy a buffet, and he joins them to view a movie. Then they play video games or

mingle with some girls until daybreak. The host usually escapes to his private suite long before then.

Doesn't sound that exciting, does it? Certainly with
such wealth, this man could travel the world, hobnob
with people of influence, support all sorts of chari-
table causes, enjoy the many cultural opportunities
around him. But he'd rather isolate himself behind
fortresslike walls and a virtually impregnable security
system, oblivious to the beauty of any of the world
outside his tiny kingdom.

All this is rather surprising when one realizes that
this man promotes a suave, sophisticated lifestyle:
quality clothes, fast cars, fine wines, gourmet foods,
elegant women, classical music, and cool jazz. That's
supposedly the picture of today's "with it" man, who,
after a full day spent making smart investments and
impeccable business decisions, is seen around town
in all the "right" places. How ironic that the inventor
of this image is sheltered inside a castle, constantly
drinking Pepsis, and eating from a rather limited menu
of fried chicken, pot roast, and sandwiches—made
only with fresh Wonder Bread.

Some have called this entrepreneur a philosopher. In
a sense they are right. A philosophy is indeed linked
to his business. A few years ago, he tried to express
it in writing. He calls it a "new morality" and right-
fully boasts about the phenomenal influence it has had
on an entire generation of college students and young
adults.

This philosophy addresses many facets of society

including individual rights, free enterprise, separation of church and state, freedom of expression, and situation ethics.

It's doubtful that many people have actually sat down and read this man's 250,000-word philosophy statement. But they have caught it's essense in his publications. An entire culture has embraced his thinking.

Frankly the philosophy is primarily a religious statement. It's drawn considerable attention from the organized church. Preachers have read about it and commented on it in their sermons. Theologians have argued its merits and debated the philosopher in his forum. The author has even admitted that his own religious background significantly influenced his thinking.

This message has one primary focus. Sex. From the beginning, this was where our social crusader fixed his attention. Puritanism was out. Freedom was in. If God made sex, then it was a sin not to enjoy it.

It originated in his youth. He was a normal, red-blooded male. Yet he felt awkward around girls. How many fellows have felt the same way. Like many males, he covered his insecurity with fantasy. He dreamed of winning young ladies with his charm, and leading them off to an intimate setting. . . .

The only problem was that instead of taming his imagination, he allowed it to grow and mature.

And then he found a way to bring his fantasies to life.

What's more significant—he brought them to life for millions of other men.

It didn't happen overnight. As a young man he spent time in the army, then went to college on the G.I. bill. After graduation, he married. He tried to find work as a cartoonist but had to settle for odd jobs in publishing. He wrote advertising copy for a Chicago department store, then promotional copy for *Esquire* magazine. Finally he became promotional manager for a small magazine-publishing company.

The work provided sufficient income to support his wife and two kids, but not near enough to finance his dream. For by now his fantasies had matured and developed. Married life had convinced him that American men were missing out on the fullness of life. They needed their horizons expanded. They needed more excitement—more, shall we say, *stimulation*.

So his spare time was occupied with the creation of a daring new publication for men. A popular magazine that would expand the boundaries of a "Puritan" society. It would include articles by some of the world's leading writers, interviews with important statesmen and thinkers, information about the good life and how to live it.

But the center piece of the publication would be a radically bold concept: a photograph—of a beautiful woman—without any clothes on.

Now "girlie" magazines had been around for many years. They were mostly low-budget publications, sold in seedy establishments. The pictures were often fuzzy shots of strippers—sad women beyond their prime.

But this new magazine had a radical concept. The centerfolds were not strippers, or professional models, or actresses. These were pictures of "the girl next door." She was pure. Wholesome. Innocent. You saw her shopping, working in the office, weeding in her garden, sunning on the beach.

The unspoken message was brash and simple. She was *available*. If you played your cards right, you could have her for an evening. No commitments required.

It was this bold, unheard-of-approach that awakened a society's sexual longing. People agreed it was time to bring sex out of the closet. Take it out of the smut shop and put it on the newsstands. Talk about it. Experience it. Why, there was nothing to be ashamed of!

Of course, such sex was without morals. The message was that marriage was not necessary—or even desirable. If two people liked each other, why not. . . .

So they did. Their philosopher assured them that they shouldn't feel guilty. He didn't (or so he claimed). He divorced his wife so he could enjoy his "freedom." He kept a private notebook, listing each of his conquests by name—more than a thousand by 1984.

No thought was given to any of the consequences of such a lifestyle.

No concern was voiced about the women who felt like nothing more than objects to be pawed over.

No one thought about the comely woman who

wasn't "stacked" right. How did she feel about this emphasis on outer beauty?

And what about taking responsibility for the untold marriages and families that were ripped apart because men chose to follow this leader and live this lifestyle? There was no admittance that there might be some physical consequences. Or that such "one-night stands" couldn't begin to replace the joy and intimacy possible in a monogamous relationship called marriage.

The only thought being promoted was self-gratification. Nothing else seemed to matter.

By now you've probably guessed that the man we're discussing is Hugh Hefner, founder of *Playboy* magazine, author of the Playboy philosophy, leader of a way of thinking that has captured a generation of men.

What you probably don't know is that Hugh Hefner grew up in a Christian home. His parents and grandparents were loyal church members who loved God and sought to please the Lord.

Young Hugh attended church every Sunday. He learned about Jesus Christ and the love he offers to all who are willing to accept it—on his terms.

Hugh Hefner didn't like the terms. He didn't want to surrender control of his life. He didn't like being confined by rules. To him, obeying Christ meant no drinking, no movies on Sundays, no bad language, and most important, no sex outside of marriage. Those restrictions seemed unreasonable.

For whatever reason, Hugh Hefner never realized

that a life dedicated to Christ is not a list of rules, but a relationship that changes one's motivations—from the inside out.

How ironic that Hugh Hefner's choice has influenced millions of others. That's always the case. Each of us, regardless of background, must choose to follow the Lord, or reject him and follow the cravings of our fleshly desires.

Whichever way we choose, it will affect the lives of others—for good or for ill.

Maybe your life won't touch millions, like Hugh Hefner. But then again, maybe it will. Will it be for the lusts of the flesh? Or for the glory of God?[3]

Coaching on a Higher Level 4

I t was the game of his life. Coach Wedemeyer wanted to win it more than any game he'd ever played or coached. Undoubtedly this was his last chance to win the title.

The Los Gatos High School football team had battled adversity, dissension, and great odds to reach the championship game of California's Central Coast Section. One year earlier, they'd lost a heartbreaker in overtime in the semifinals. The team that had defeated them, Saint Francis, went on to win its third consecutive sectional title. Los Gatos had never even reached the finals of the tournament.

This year the team was less talented and not even picked to win its league. They'd lost the opening game of the season. The assistant coaches were complaining about the work load and privately wondering if it was time for Coach Wedemeyer to step down. The players were trying to run a highly complex offense without the all-stars who had graduated last year. Almost everyone believed this was a rebuilding year.

But Charlie Wedemeyer had never backed away from a challenge. Though only five feet, eight inches tall, he was an outstanding football player in high school. In fact, he was voted outstanding athlete of the 1960s in the state of Hawaii. He went on to play football at Michigan State University. His coach, the legendary Duffy Dougherty, noted that though he weighed only 175 pounds, "he'd take on a couple of two-hundred-and-forty-pounders and knock their blocks off." His senior season, he returned to Hawaii to play in the Hula Bowl All-Star game.

In 1972 Charlie went to work at Los Gatos High School near San Jose. He taught math and was assistant football coach. In 1977 his dream of becoming head coach came true. And what teams he produced! Over the next nine years, the school won seven league titles. There were seventy-seven wins and only seventeen defeats. But the big dream—the sectional championship—had eluded them.

Los Gatos's best chance to win the title had evaporated in that semifinal loss to Saint Francis. As the new season opened, there was grumbling among the ranks, but the coach rallied his squad, and they won their second game to start a new winning streak.

The team's powerful offense began to function like a machine. They outscored the rest of their opponents to win another league title. The winning continued throughout the play-offs. And now, against all odds, they were playing for the championship. Their opponents: Saint Francis—the team that had ruined their dream the previous fall; the school that had won three straight sectional titles.

It's a moving story, yet one that could easily be told in many other communities around the country. More than two-hundred high-school football teams win state championships each year. Certainly a number of them would qualify as underdogs or Cinderella stories. It's not *that* unusual.

What makes this story different is Charlie Wedemeyer. For as this determined head coach prepared to work his final game, he was immobilized in a golf cart, attached to a respirator, and unable to talk. His wife read his lips and relayed his decisions. Despite these incredible handicaps, he called every play.

It was a miracle that Charlie was alive, much less coaching a championship football team. He is a victim of Amyotrophic lateral sclerosis (ALS). It's better known as Lou Gehrig's Disease—named after the famous New York Yankee baseball player. Nine years before this momentous game, Charlie was given only twelve to eighteen months to live.

ALS is a disease that attacks the nerve cells and causes the voluntary muscles to atrophy. There is no cure, and no hope of recovery.

At first Charlie felt some loss of feeling. He dropped things and had unexplained stumbles. Gradually it got worse. Charlie's wife, Lucy, and their two children had to watch his once finely tuned body deteriorate. His arms stopped working. He couldn't walk without assistance.

However, the disease doesn't touch the brain. Charlie's mind was as sharp as ever. It's just that his body would no longer obey the brain's commands.

Initially, Charlie and Lucy didn't want to face the awful implications of their situation. Charlie tried to keep up his normal activities. But he required constant attention—for his own safety. He was frustrated that he could no longer do routine things—like write on the blackboard or shave. His speech slurred, and it became harder to understand him. For a man who was a perfectionist, it was hard to admit that he was no longer in control of his life.

The school system decided not to rehire Charlie as a teacher. However, he persuaded the principal that he could still function as head football coach. Some supporters gave him a golf cart to help him get around the field.

Steadily his body deteriorated. Nights were the hardest. Breathing became difficult. Phlegm accumulated. He was so afraid of choking to death that he could not sleep. He worried about the mounting health bills. He agonized as he saw the strain his illness placed on his loved ones. Lucy worked valiantly as a real estate broker, nurse to her husband, and mother of two teenagers.

The fighter in Charlie wanted to live. The burden he saw on his loved ones made him want to die. Only when Lucy told him, "We'd rather have you this way than not at all," did he have the courage to keep fighting.

But still the fear plagued him. What good was it to live when you can't enjoy life? Lucy told him that he could speak to God. But somehow that didn't help.

Gradually his condition got worse. Breathing and eating became more difficult. His weight dropped below one-hundred pounds. One day, a nurse spent eight hours trying to get him to swallow some juice—but he couldn't. The situation was desperate.

When the relief nurse arrived, she didn't know what to do—except pray. She placed her hands on Charlie's chest and started asking God for his help. "It was like a presence came into the room," Charlie says today. When the nurse finished, Charlie felt assured that God would do a miracle. The first miracle was that he immediately ate two bowls of soup.

Lucy hurried home when she learned of the good news. And that caring nurse led the couple in a prayer of commitment to Jesus Christ. Immediately, Charlie's greatest fear—the fear of death was lifted. He knew his eternal destination.

Now Charlie realized that he had a choice. He could continue to worry about his problems, which were out of his control; or he could turn them over to a loving God. He chose to trust God. For the first time in months, he could sleep at night.

Soon that decision was tested. A few months later, Charlie stopped breathing and was rushed to the hospital. An emergency tracheotomy was required to save his life.

"I never felt so scared in my life," Charlie says about that day. "I wouldn't have made it, except that I could pray and review the Scripture verses I'd memorized. That was all I could do, but it was enough."

Because of the operation, Charlie could breath only on a respirator. He could no longer talk. He required around-the-clock nursing care. It took a minimum of two hours to prepare him when he left the house. Still, he insisted on coaching one more season. Under his determined leadership, he inspired his team to reach the summit, and thus, they found themselves, the underdogs, playing for the championship.

It was a classic struggle. Saint Francis scored first, but Los Gatos tied the game at six. Then in the third quarter, the Wildcats scored the go-ahead touchdown. Coach Wedemeyer called for a two-point conversion, and it succeeded. Saint Francis battled back in the fourth quarter, scoring another touchdown. But they missed the two-point conversion. Los Gatos led 14-12.

Then with forty seconds remaining, Saint Francis lined up to attempt a short field goal that would win the game.

Los Gatos blocked the kick.

Charlie and his team had won the championship!

It was the pinnacle of the school's athletic history. And it was Charlie's last game as head football coach.

But he was still alive, and he wanted to be useful. It wasn't his nature to sit idly at home.

For a time, Charlie wondered how God could possibly use him in his paralyzed condition. "I can't walk. I can't talk. I don't even know much about the Bible. How can I do anything for the Lord?" he wondered.

He didn't realize that a new career was about to emerge. First, Los Gatos High School paid him to be a consultant to the football team. The players often spent hours with him after practices, talking about their football technique, and about the things of God. His home became a constant beehive of activity as kids visited and looked to him for counsel.

Then Charlie was invited to speak to a high school camp. As his nurse, Linda, interpreted, he told the teenagers about his football career. And about how God helped him endure his illness. "All my football honors and all my awards couldn't help me," he said. "Only my relationship with the Lord saved me."

The response was phenomenal. Youngsters swarmed around him and told him how God had challenged them to change—because of his message. One mother wrote several months later: "When my child got home from camp, he was a different person. I wondered how long it would last. Well, he's still different, and it's because of what he learned from you."

That talk led to numerous invitations to speak at churches. Everywhere he went, people responded. He

spoke to teenagers at a boys' ranch. Afterward a boy
wrote him: "Before you came, I worshiped Satan. But
since hearing your testimony, I realize there is a God.
Thank you for showing me."

A documentary was made of Charlie and Lucy's
story. It was shown on public television. One man in
a Seattle hotel room saw it. His million-dollar business
had failed, and his wife had left him. He was preparing to commit suicide—until he saw this story, and
realized he still had a reason to live.

Charlie went to visit other ALS patients. Early in
his illness, he couldn't stand to be around other victims. It was too depressing. It reminded him of his
hopeless condition. But *now* he had a message of hope.
There was reason to live—reason to thank God.

After speaking to a men's breakfast in Redding, a
local football coach stood up and said, "Charlie, you
may not be head coach any more. But I want you to
know that you're still coaching. Only now you're
coaching a much bigger game, with a lot more players,
on a higher level."

So today Charlie proudly smiles and announces to
all that he's an assistant coach—to the greatest Head
Coach. "My goal now is to keep coaching on a higher
level!"[4]

Caught in the Conflict 5

D̲o you like criticism? Most likely you do not. How do you feel when someone you love is verbally blasted—unfairly, you believe? Do you want to defend him or her? Or would you rather retreat and hide until the storm blows over?

Leilani hated conflict. She avoided it at all costs. Unfortunately, her husband thrived on it. In fact, he was the object of intense media attention from the national press—much of it negative. If Leilani didn't learn how to handle the criticism of her husband, it would ruin her.

In fact, it almost did.

Born in southeast Wyoming and raised on a farm, Leilani met her future husband in high school. She was the only girl he ever dated. Together they talked about their dreams. He wanted to do something to make America a better place to live. His plan was to attend the University of Wyoming, go to law school, and ultimately become governor of Wyoming.

Together they went off to college and were married during their sophomore year. As so often happens, it was only after the marriage ceremony that Leilani discovered how different they were. And those differences caused her a lot of pain.

Basically, her husband was ambitious. He wanted to push forward and make things happen, even if it made others uncomfortable. He was decisive, and never looked back once he made a decision.

Leilani, however, never wanted to upset anyone. She could support people who had totally opposite viewpoints. She was unwilling to take a stand that might offend someone.

The husband was a risk taker. Leilani wanted to play it safe. He enjoyed teasing a friend, sometimes— Leilani thought—unmercifully. She shriveled under such kidding and wouldn't think of poking fun at anyone. He enjoyed a rousing debate on any subject, particularly politics. She hated arguments of any kind. He wouldn't think of retreat. She inevitably avoided uncomfortable conversations.

Leilani believed that the Bible teaching about wives submitting to their husbands meant she had no voice in his decisions. She had to follow him whether or not she agreed with him. Afterall, that's how Christians acted, she thought.

However, by not voicing her true feelings, she became a miserable woman, full of pent-up anger and frustration. But she never showed it, for she remained placid on the outside.

It didn't take long for Leilani's politically inspired husband to make his mark. They were off to Washington where he served as assistant to a senator he helped elect. Then there were appointments to important posts in the Washington bureaucracy. But Leilani couldn't enjoy her husband's success. She knew little about his work and made little effort to find out about it.

This is not to imply that Leilani was an unimaginative, lazy woman. Not at all. She had a master's degree. She was a talented seamstress. She kept a beautiful home. She volunteered for community activities. And she was a dedicated mother. It's just that she couldn't stand any kind of conflict.

For example, dinnertime often produced tension. Her husband loved to instigate lively discussions with their children as they ate. As the kids grew, the topics for debate expanded. Often there was heated dialogue as her husband challenged statements and everyone was encouraged to express and defend his or her views. Many a time, Leilani left the table in tears and retreated to the basement, while the rest of the family finished their talks.

The internal turmoil affected Leilani's health. For

four years she struggled with an undiagnosed muscle
disease that left her so weak that she spent much of
her time resting on a sofa. Naturally, it was frustrating
to her husband and put strain on their relationship.

Occasionally when she had the energy, Leilani attended a Bible study. It was there the tide began to
turn. She learned that her silence did not equal submission. Rather it was a symptom of disrespect—for
herself and her husband. It was a mask that covered
up her true feelings.

But how could she change? She found that she often
learned the truth about herself through mental pictures. God seemed to speak to her through vivid im-
ages that portrayed her problems.

One morning, after the Bible study on submission,
she saw a picture in her mind that she instantly rec-
ognized as representative of her marriage. It contained
two rowboats, each with a seat and a set of oars. The
two boats were connected by a thick rope. She realized
that these two boats represented their lives. They were
attached, but Leilani was free to stay behind her husband, or speed on ahead, or come alongside and poke
him with an oar.

As she viewed the scene, she saw these words: GET
INTO HIS BOAT. Panic filled her. She didn't like the fact
that there was only one set of oars—and her husband
would be rowing. Yet this picture showed her what
was missing in their marriage. Their lives were not
integrated. She didn't know what he was thinking, or
where he was hurting. It was much more comfortable

rowing her own boat than being in the same boat. They'd have to be a team, working together for the same goals.

That choice was a hard one, but she knew she had to make it if she was ever going to find peace in her home. She tearfully told her husband the news that she was getting into his boat. After a moment of reflection, he answered, "Glub, glub, glub!" Leilani was devastated. She should have expected a touch of humor, but she didn't like it. She wasn't sure she wanted to trust her life to him.

However, time would prove those words prophetic.

Getting into her husband's boat took care of the issue of teamwork. But it didn't deal with her own inner turmoil. And for what was coming, she would need a source of peace.

The answer came through another vivid picture. This time, it was of a large stove with huge burners and several large pots on them—the size one would use to cook chili for fifty people. The lids were dancing on top of the pots, and puffs of steam were rising to the ceiling. It seemed to Leilani that her purpose in life was to keep the lids on those pots.

After frantically trying to hold down the lids, she reached down and turned off the heat. Any cook knows that will quickly settle things down. However, as she began to relax, she saw a giant hand—and somehow she knew it was God's hand—reach down and turn the heat up as high as it could go. Soon the lids were dancing with a loud, rattling noise and threatening to fly completely off the pots.

Leilani doubled her efforts to keep the lids on. Then she heard these words: "If you would let *me* cleanse those pots, you wouldn't have to worry about keeping the lids on."

Incredulous, she asked, "What's in the pots?"

"Anger" was the answer. She immediately dismissed that, for if there was one thing that didn't describe this woman, it was anger. She was the most patient mother you'd ever seen. She rarely yelled at her children. She always had a smile for her neighbor. She meekly accepted the surly abuse of an irritable store clerk.

Yet she couldn't erase the picture from her mind. Gradually she began to realize that her anger was surpressed. She was angry at God for not healing her, angry at her husband for pushing the children, angry at her brother for the vicious fights they'd had as kids. But God was willing to cleanse her of that anger—if she would only admit it and let him do the scouring.

Once she did that, she began to experience a wonderful truth. God provides all that we need in the midst of conflict—peace, patience, kindness, wisdom, even joy.

Why were those two lessons so important to this woman? Because she was going to face more conflict than most of us can even imagine. Her husband would be thrust into the public spotlight and vilified and

mocked by TV and newspaper commentators and political cartoonists.

If you follow politics, you might recognize Leilani's
husband. His name is James Watt. For three years, he
was Secretary of the Interior in President Reagan's
cabinet.

President Reagan wanted the country to develop energy independence. James Watt followed that policy
by opening up multiple-use lands for evaluation of
natural resources. He proposed a leasing program for
off-shore oil and gas.

Environmental groups vociferously attacked these
plans. They argued in favor of protecting more land.
Save our resources, they argued. *Don't endanger the en-
vironment.* Secretary Watt tried to demonstrate the bal-
ance of his policies. He was improving the National
Park System and insisting on stringent safeguards
where there was oil and gas exploration. But few
seemed to hear his arguments.

Rarely has a cabinet member been so controversial.
James Watt was featured on covers of *TIME* and *News-
week.* Cartoonists loved to draw his bald pate and
thick glasses. Hardly a day passed when he wasn't the
subject of some controversy.

He made enemies of music fans when he banned
rock music—including the Beach Boys—from the July 4
celebration on the Washington Mall. He was harshly
criticized for a letter to Israel's ambassador, urging
Jewish support for U.S. energy development policies.

He was ridiculed for stating the racial and political makeup of his coal commission.

How did Leilani handle such constant pressure? Her natural inclination was to avoid it. It hurt deeply to see her husband ridiculed. It would be easy to say these were his problems and turn away.

But God had shown her the need to support her husband. He needed someone to help bear his burdens. He needed a place of refuge beyond the public clamor, a place only she could provide.

What Leilani really wanted to do was set the public record straight. If she could just call the newspaper editors and television producers and tell them the facts! But she knew she could never change media perspective.

However, *she could support her husband in prayer.* So, Leilani became an intercessor. Every morning as her husband went to work, she spent several hours praying on his behalf, feeling the pain of his critics, and claiming for him promises of Scripture—for wisdom, patience, insight, and strength.

Some people might say Leilani's prayers weren't very important. Certainly she could have supported her husband in more practical ways. But James Watt would disagree. As a Christian, he experienced the strength of his wife's faith and commitment in the midst of public pressure. He admits that he could never have survived those three harrowing years without his wife's love and support.

James Watt likes to tell people that God gave him a new wife. Not another woman, but a changed woman. A woman who no longer ran from conflict, but found victory in its midst.[5]

Who Said Life Was Fair? 6

Butch had so much going his way. At the age of twenty-two he had a business degree from Indiana University. He'd been offered a management position with Proctor and Gamble. He was earning a handsome salary as a professional basketball player. Yet, he was virtually broke—and it wasn't his fault.

In high school Butch was one of those guys who could do it all. He was an All-State football and basketball player. He got good grades. He went to church every Sunday.

He also was willing to shoulder responsibility. At the age of twelve, his father had abandoned the family. As the oldest of seven children, Butch became the man of the house.

55

Pressure didn't bother him either. He hit the winning basket in the final seconds of the NIT championship game one year. The next year, he made the winning shot in overtime to propel Indiana to the Big Ten championship.

But all of this talent and experience couldn't prepare him for the stark moment of truth when he learned the bank had a lien on his home and his financial affairs were in ruins.

No one plans to get into a financial mess, and certainly Butch didn't either. And what made his situation so exasperating was that he was in this predicament because he was trying to do something right. He was trying to help someone in need.

Still, the numbers spelled financial ruin. He was advised to declare bankruptcy. Certainly, he had no choice. No one would blame him. After all, it wasn't even his fault.

But Butch had another idea.

The problem had started when Butch signed his first contract to play basketball for the Los Angeles Lakers. As you might expect, when someone so young suddenly is rewarded with a nice sum of money, there are people who want a piece of that pie. So it was with Butch.

A friend—no, that's not quite right; a *relative* came by and asked for a loan. It seems this person was down on his luck. He needed some help to get back on his feet. He didn't want a handout—just some help starting a little business. And really, Butch didn't need to give him a dime. If he'd only cosign on a bank loan, the man would be in business.

It seemed like the right thing to do. God had blessed Butch, and this was an opportunity to do something to help someone who wasn't as fortunate.

Visits were made to two local banks, in case one turned them down. Applications were made for loans. When one of the loans was approved, Butch cosigned, guaranteeing to repay the money in the event his relative was unable to do so. Of course Butch was promised that the payments would be made. No problem. I won't bother you again. Thanks so much for your help. You're a great guy. Good luck with the Lakers.

There was one other piece of business before Butch departed for training camp. He put a down payment on his dream house. Now he had some roots. A place to go to in the off-season and when his basketball career was finished. His brother agreed to live in the house and be caretaker while he was gone.

Some months later Butch returned home. His brother didn't know how to tell him. . . . He *should* have forwarded all the mail, but he didn't want to disturb Butch. It seems these two banks were sending notices.

"Two banks!" said Butch. "I signed a loan only at one bank."

A check was made, and it turned out someone had forged Butch's signature at the second bank. Then he went to visit this relative to find out why he wasn't making the payments. That's when he learned the awful truth. The money was gone. The man promised he'd catch up on the payments. He'd pay it all back—just give him time. But Butch knew better. The man would never be able to pay him back.

The banks wanted their money back now. They suggested—no, *demanded*—his house. But that wouldn't clear up the debt. Butch didn't want to wipe out the one real asset he had.

He suggested an alternative. He showed them a payment plan that would repay the loans eventually, though not within the original time frame. The banks said *no!*

The interest on those loans was astronomical. Two percent above prime. At that time prime was 20 percent. The interest alone for one year was in five figures.

So what was he to do? They didn't prepare you for this kind of problem in college. Where could he go for some decent financial advice?

Butch went to his Bible and began reading in earnest.

He couldn't believe how much the Scriptures had to say about money. One statement nailed him between the eyes:

It is poor judgment to countersign another's note,
to become responsible for his debts (Prov. 17:18, TLB).

Five times similar warnings are given in Proverbs. If only he had paid attention to this sooner. God had wanted to protect him from just this kind of a mess.

What else did the Good Book have to say?

Evil men borrow and "cannot pay it back!" But the good man returns what he owes with some extra besides (Ps. 37:21, TLB).

There was no question that Butch had an obligation to pay off his debt. Regardless of who was at fault, the responsibility was his. Already he'd heard advice about bankruptcy. That would be the easy way out. It was legal. He could clean the slate and start over. But that wasn't God's way.

The Scriptures had another important warning:

Bring all the tithes into the storehouse so that there will be food enough in my Temple; if you do, I will open up the windows of heaven for you and pour out a blessing so great you won't have room enough to take it in!" (Mal. 3:10, TLB).

Butch made a critical decision. "No matter what, I would give 10 percent of whatever I make to our local church, missionary work, and local charities."

So some important lessons were being learned, but the problem of repaying the loans remained. He was determined to fulfill his obligations, but how could he do so with the constant harassment from the banks? He needed time.

There was a bright side to this predicament. Butch realized he was only twenty-two years old. He could survive. In fact, it would be far better to learn these lessons now than if he was forty or fifty. For that he gave thanks to God.

At this point, the legal system provided some help. The law allows a person in this circumstance to reorganize. The debt is not forgiven, but a plan is developed to pay the money back—and the creditors are ordered to stop harassing the debtor. That was the procedure Butch followed.

After filing the necessary papers, Butch began thinking of ways to retire that debt. There was his house. He had recently married, and his wife loved the home. Together, they agreed that they would have to give it up temporarily. So they rented the home out and moved into a tiny apartment. The difference each month was applied to the debt.

Then Butch's basketball career lasted longer than many expected. He wasn't earning an extravagant salary, but what he made was frugally managed. It took four years, but Butch paid back every single dollar of his obligation.

Butch is no longer playing basketball. While he was in the NBA, he determined that he would not be like 80 percent of the other pro basketball players, who are dead broke five years after their careers are completed. He prepared for a second career. He did marketing research and learned what businesses would work well in his community. He systematically laid out a ten-year plan. Two years into the plan, he would be able to make it without pro ball.

Today the bankers are glad to see Butch when he walks into their offices. He is a respected businessman. He is known as a man of integrity—a man who's word is good. And that counts for a lot these days.

That doesn't mean that the scars from his experience are completely healed. Butch admits he learned some very important lessons about finances. But there's a principle that supercedes even those lessons—something that will no doubt effect the rest of his life and the lives of his children.

You see, there's one fact we've neglected to mention so far in this story—the identity of the man for whom Butch cosigned the loan.

That man was his father.

Yes, he was the man who deserted his family when Butch was just twelve years old.

Butch soberly states this important truth: "My father showed me what happens when you take the quick and easy way out. It doesn't get you anywhere. I've learned that you only get out of life what you put into it."

And what motivates him to take the narrow road of obedience to God's ways? "Remember," he answers, "our faith in Jesus Christ is the only thing that's going to last forever."[6]

Good Grades or More Fun? 7

It sounds like a contradiction. You can go to college and work hard for good grades; or you can have a great time—at the cost of those grades. But you can't have both.

Or can you?

Many of you have made plans for college. You're looking at a year or two of junior college or trade school. Or four years at a college or university. Perhaps you're even planning for a master's or doctorate. Anyway you look at it, there's a lot of school ahead. And you can't take it lightly, for your performance in school may well determine your earning power later.

So you know you have to work hard; yet, you don't want to sacrifice the good times. Is it possible to achieve good grades and still have some fun in the process?

Steve Douglass asked those questions while he attended the Massachusetts Institute of Technology (MIT). After he earned his bachelor's degree, he went to Harvard Business School and earned a master's. At Harvard he graduated in the top 2 percent of his class. Still, he found time for a wide variety of activities.

So how did he do it? Was he a genius? Well, Steve is no dummy, but I wouldn't say his intelligence is way above average either. Maybe he studied more than anyone else? But if that was true, he wouldn't have had time for basketball, fraternity functions, student politics, dating, and several other campus activities.

In fact, Steve learned that neither intelligence nor the amount of study time affect grades as much as you might think. Some students study six hours a day, yet their grades are no better than other students, with similar IQ, who study no more than two hours a day. He found that some people with high IQs actually get poorer grades because they don't understand the secret of success in school.

It's amazing that although they may spend ten thousand dollars a year (and more) on a college education, many students do not know how to get the most for their money. Steve didn't either, but he was determined to find out. As a result, he learned there was one rule that governs success in school. Master it, and you can get better grades *and* have more fun.

What's that rule? It's actually a fundamental principle of economics. It was first identified and stated by an Italian economist and sociologist, Vilfredo Pareto.

Maybe that sounds like an unusual place to find the secret of studying, but it works, as you will see.

Sometimes it's the simplest, most obvious things that we miss. Steve noted that some of his classmates skipped class frequently. He then observed a pattern. Those who tended to miss classes generally got poorer grades. In other words, those who diligently attended class got better grades.

His observation was supported by a ten-year study of undergraduates at the University of Michigan. It found that students who attended 79 percent of classes or less ended up with a low C average. Those who attended 90 percent and above scored above a B average.

And catch this: students who attended class and sat in the first three rows got significantly higher grades!

Why is this so significant? Steve explains: "The vast majority of classes are relevant to what the instructor expects you to learn. Think about it—attending class gives you thirty or more exposures to the subject. And repetition is crucial to learning."

Granted that going to class does imply that a person is doing more than just sitting there. But just how does someone get the most out of class? Steve discovered that the single most important thing he could do was ask this question in the first class session: *What is the course objective?* What essential things does the professor want you to learn this term? That will give you valuable insight that will help you know where to focus your attention. If the professor doesn't tell the class this information, then the student has every right to ask.

Another observation Steve made concerned the taking of notes. Many students spend their class time furiously writing down everything the professor says. They proudly display pages of notes for each class session. But Steve discovered that such diligent activity was counterproductive. Those students spend so much time writing that they often missed the most important lessons. He found he usually got better results with just one page of notes.

The principle he applied is what he calls *aggressive listening*. How does one listen aggressively? First, he's curious, alert, aware of all that's being said and going on. Second, he's constantly asking questions such as, "Is this information valuable?" "How does this fit the course objective?" and "Do I need to probe deeper?"

The information Steve gained by scanning and asking told him where to focus his attention and explore deeper. He put these points into an acrostic: **SAFE:**

Scan

Ask

Focus

Explore

He applied this "SAFE" outline on his class notes. On the top two-thirds of a page, he would jot down the key points of a professor's teaching. Then on the bottom third, he jotted down reactions and questions that he would ask the professor. Finally, as the class ended, he wrote a summary of the lesson learned in that class session. Those summary statements proved a valuable means of review prior to tests.

Another aspect of Steve's school habits concerned showing the professor what he had learned. A simple motto reflected his attitude: IT'S NOT JUST WHAT YOU KNOW BUT WHAT YOU SHOW. In other words, you don't get graded on what's in your head but on what you show the professor.

There are only three ways to show what you know: *class participation, homework,* and *exams.* Steve's organized note-taking process helped him interact intelligently during class discussions. As for homework, he always tried to hand it in on time. And on exams, he always went through a test twice. First, he answered all the questions to which he instantly knew the answer. If he got stuck, he quickly moved on to the next question and went back to it later. Then he answered every question to the fullest, making sure he didn't leave out any pertinent information.

These sound like common-sense details, but many students don't follow these basics. And they struggle with school.

Steve made one other observation: he noted that some students had trouble managing their time. He would see some studying late into the night, drinking coffee to try to stay awake. How much did they learn in that condition? It made more sense if they would sleep when they were tired and study when they were most alert.

Steve decided that he would consciously try to use his strengths to maximum advantage. One of his strengths is that he does his best work in the morning. So he rarely studied past nine o'clock at night. Instead, he got up at five in the morning and found he did several times more work than when he was tired.

Steve also found that he worked better standing up instead of sitting. So he built a stand-up work desk. Sounds unusual, but it worked for him. And that's the point. Why study the same way as everyone else, if you have methods that work better for you?

Have you figured out Steve's rule for getting better grades and having more fun in school? In economics, it's known as the Pareto Principle. For college students, Steve calls it the 80/20 Rule. It says:

80 percent of the benefit from school can be derived from doing the right 20 percent of the activity well.

That's the secret to success. And it really works! In fact, that principle has helped him succeed after graduation. Today, Steve is executive vice-president of a multinational organization that employs more than sixteen thousand people.

There's one additional truth Steve learned in college, one that goes far beyond systems of study. During his senior year at MIT, he won the prestigious Karl Taylor Compton Award. As he was walking up to the podium to receive it, he could hear himself thinking in his mind, "So what! Big deal!" Here he'd achieved such great success as a student. If, in his moment of glory, it was no big deal, then it was going to be a long life.

That was the event that led to his commitment to Christ during the summer. Going into Harvard as a graduate student, he had a new perspective about school. He realized that God was the ultimate source of wisdom and knowlege. And even more, he found God was the source of peace.

That latter lesson was learned as a result of his first exam at Harvard. He had spent six weeks in school. He had prepared as well as he could for the test, but when he emerged from the examination hall, he knew he hadn't done well.

It was a frustrating moment as he returned to his room. As he tells it, "I remembered that the Bible says that the results of a person's relationship with God should include love, joy, and peace. Well, I certainly wasn't experiencing peace. So I prayed, 'God, I'm not asking for any favors on the exam. But would you please give me your peace.' "

Steve today laughs as he remembers that God answered both of his prayers. He didn't give Steve any favors on the exam. ("Next time I prayed more intelligently!" he jokes.) And he gave Steve total peace within minutes.

That lesson—learning to experience God's peace in the midst of pressure—is the most valuable lesson Steve learned in college. It's one that he continues to use while wrestling with complex problems in his work. While he's applying the 80/20 Rule—focusing his energy on the 20 percent of activities that will yield 80 percent of the result.[7]

Searching for Freedom 8

Have you ever thought about what it would be like to be totally free? I mean *no* responsibility. No parents looking over your shoulder. No classes to attend or grades to worry about. No job to force you out of bed two hours earlier than you'd like. And no concern about where you'll find your next meal.

Few ever have that chance—to be their own boss, to do their own thing, to be free of all worry. Well, almost all.

Actually, the more you think about it, the more unrealistic it sounds. But one person came about as close to fulfilling that dream as may be humanly possible. His name is Robin Lee Graham.

School was like a prison to Robin. But the ocean—

that was different. From the age of ten, when his father bought him an eight-foot dinghy, sailing was an escape from restrictions. When Robin was fourteen, his father sold his business, bought a boat, and sailed to the South Pacific. For a year, the family explored the South Sea islands.

When they returned to California, Robin found it even more difficult to sit still in school. He couldn't forget the feel of the sea gently rocking him to sleep. The joy of exploring island reefs. How the native girls ran along the golden beaches, their arms filled with fresh fruit and exotic flowers. Or sitting for hours at night and staring at the stars.

The contrast was too great. He loved handling a sextant, not trying to improve his spelling. Fast-food hamburgers tasted flat compared to coconut milk and mangoes. How could he be content in a California classroom, trying to learn meaningless subjects, when he was already a seasoned sailor? How could anyone expect him to go on to college and graduate to an office, sit behind a desk, and be fulfilled?

A dream began to grow. A dream that had him quitting school and sailing. How far could he go? Alone—without any parents or authority figures?

Perhaps he'd sail around the world.

Of course, let's be realistic. He didn't have the money to buy a boat. He couldn't just up and leave. Though he tried.

Robin's father bought a new boat, and together they sailed to Hawaii. There he was enrolled in high school.

He found two friends who loved sailing as much as he did. The three of them invested their combined savings— about one hundred dollars—in an old sixteen-foot aluminum lifeboat. They added a keel, built a mast, and found some old sails. Then one Friday, they skipped school and set sail for the island of Lanai.

They'd just left Ala Wai Harbor when the wind rose and soon they were tossing wildly in the midst of thirty-foot waves. They were feared lost. The Coast Guard conducted a search. Miraculously they managed to bring their battered boat to land.

The crazy stunt produced headlines. Taxpayers were angry at the thousands of dollars spent trying to rescue three irresponsible kids. They were guilty of breaking a federal law that prohibits reckless operation of a vehicle that endangers any person. But the incident only fueled Robin's desire to escape from civilization.

Escape to what? He wasn't sure. He only knew that he wanted to be his own man, free of all rules and regulations.

Robin's father gave him that chance. Perhaps his son's near tragic escapade convinced him that it was better to let the boy go. Back home in Southern California, he bought Robin a twenty-four-foot sloop called *Dove*. Together they spent a month fitting the boat for the high seas.

Robin made one promise to his father. He would try to sail as far as he could—around the world, if possible. And so, one summer morning, at the age of sixteen, he set sail on the first leg of what would become a five-year, solo journey.

What a trip it was. Full of adventure. Of exploration of new lands and different cultures. Of life-threatening battles against storms and raging seas.

And we mustn't forget romance. In the Fiji Islands, Robin met Patti, a California girl born just fifty miles from his home. They frolicked on the lush islands, enjoying total freedom. If it were not for his commitment to his father, he might well have settled there in paradise.

But that only begins to show that no freedom is total—or should we say that every freedom has its price? Yes, Robin had to pay.

At times, the cost was intense, almost insane loneliness. He'd see a beautiful sunset, or a phosphorescent sea, and have no one to share it with. His moods fluctuated with the weather—up on sunny days, gloomy when there were clouds. The depression went deepest when he hit the doldrums—those spots of ocean where no wind blew—when the boat might not move ten miles in a day. At times he so yearned for a human voice that he'd talk into his tape recorder, then play it back.

There was the price of weariness—the long nights without sleep, as the winds shifted and he had to make sure the boat stayed on course. There were little worries—the stove malfunctioning, the supply of kerosene being depleted. Then there were the big worries—knowing a minute error in his navigation could leave him hopelessly lost at sea, or when storms tossed the boat around and threatened to send it to a deep, liquid grave.

You don't feel so brave then. You know loved ones are home, worrying about your safety. You can practically see the newspaper headlines, telling about a boy lost at sea.

Ultimately, this courageous youngster had to face death. He had to realize his human limitations. Once he was caught in a ferocious storm on the Indian Ocean off the coast of the great Island of Malagasy (Madagascar). At the height of the storm, a vicious wave snapped the mast off like it was a twig. He was forced to stay awake for nearly forty-eight hours, trying to save his boat. But it seemed hopeless. It was then that he prayed the first prayer of his life: "God, or whoever you are, please help me."

Almost immediately, the storm began to subside. Exhausted, he fell into a deep sleep. When he awoke, the seas were calm.

With his prayer answered, Robin promptly jury-rigged a mast and proceeded toward the coast off South Africa—and forgot about the God who calmed the sea.

Five years after he sailed out of Long Beach Harbor, Robin returned home from his journey a hero. His trip caught the imagination of the country. He was the youngest person to circumnavigate the globe alone. For a time, he was featured on television, in newspapers, in *National Geographic*. He had married Patti, and he had fulfilled his dream. At twenty-one, he had it all.

And he had nothing.

The freedom he longed for was gone. There was tension with his parents, who did not approve of his marriage. There was embarrassing attention from the press who asked questions he didn't want to answer. There was a nagging concern about his future. Now what would he do with the rest of his life? College? A job? Another adventure?

He was depressed.

He started drinking excessively to escape his predicament.

He entertained thoughts of suicide.

He wondered if there was a place to which he could escape. A place where he and his wife and his daughter could live off the land, away from civilization. Where they'd be free from the crowds and the claustrophobic feeling he experienced in school and the city.

He had tasted freedom—but it did not last. His depression grew out of the realization that he could never experience permanent freedom. There was always a price to pay—always some limitation—some restriction.

The answer did not come quickly. It was a process. Through some friends, Robin and Patti were introduced to Jesus Christ. They were leery about religion. They didn't willingly accept the invitations to visit church, but they were drawn by the quality of life in their friends. And they were open, willing to consider the facts, to investigate the things of God.

To that tentative step, God responded. As they read from the New Testament, they found that the words of Jesus made sense. They realized that they had a choice—to try to run their own lives, or to allow God to take over.

As far as their immediate future, they decided to homestead in the mountains of Montana. As they drove into the state, Patti exclaimed about the spectacular scenery, "What a fantastic artist has designed all this—God, I mean."

That's when Robin prayed the second prayer of his life. It was a simple statement of surrender. A request for understanding. A willingness to obey him. A desire to let God take over and direct their lives.

Several years later, Robin recalled that moment. "We immediately felt an absolutely wonderful sense of freedom, such a lightness of heart and spirit. . . . We laughed together until we cried—not tears of pain or sorrow or solemnity, but the kind of tears people shed when they come home after a long absence."

At last, Robin had found the answer to his deep longing for freedom. It had nothing to do with escape from responsibility. It wasn't solitude on the high seas or living deep in the Montana wilderness. Rather, it was a realization of who he was. A sense that his life had significance. That there was a reason for being alive.[8]

Aftermath of Terror 9

Lee Kinney leaned back in her seat and watched the country pass by. At last she was getting her wish—a fresh start!

Until her graduation from high school, Lee's life could best be termed as miserable. She grew up in a cramped row house in an ethnic section of Philadelphia. By day, her father was a painter. At night, he retreated to his basement and drank himself into oblivion.

After several hours, her dad would emerge from the cellar in a rage and proceed to beat the nearest family members. Lee and her four sisters frequently went to school with concealed bruises from their father's rampage the night before.

Now that she had graduated, Lee wanted to move

as far away from her father as possible. She talked her mother into going with her and bought a bus ticket. Her destination: San Francisco.

She imagined how her new life would be. Her older sister lived in Frisco and had told her about the wonderful opportunities in "The City." Most of all, she looked forward to no more pain. She knew God would take care of her.

And at first, it appeared she was right. Lee found a job as a secretary for a sailboat manufacturer. She volunteered for the USO, which sponsored activities for servicemen in the Bay area. There she was able to use some of her organizational and acting skills—and meet some nice young men.

Lee Kinney had it all now. She was three-thousand miles removed from her brutal father. She had a good job. And she was living in one of the finest cities, full of many cultural and social opportunities.

One night, Lee worked late at the office with two other secretaries to help finish the paperwork for a large order of boats. Lee mentioned a movie she planned to watch on TV after they were finished. The salesman supervising the order suggested they pick up some pizzas and go watch the movie at his place.

When they were done, Lee followed the salesman in her car and assumed the other two secretaries would follow shortly with the pizzas. Lee arrived at a run-down mobile home. Once inside the salesman overpowered her.

Details aren't necessary here. It was an awful ex-

perience. A nightmare. Once the rapist had satisfied
his lust, Lee tore out of the house, jumped into her car
and drove off.

A few blocks from home, she parked. "Why me?"
she cried out to God. "Where were *you* when this
happened? Why didn't you warn me? Haven't I suf-
fered enough?"

Lee told no one about the attack, and tried to bury
the memories. But in the following weeks, she began
to feel sick. Sore throat. Nausea. She probably had the
flu. It was going around, her friends said. So she visited a clinic.

"As far as I can tell, you're pregnant," said the doctor. A blood test confirmed his diagnosis.

The news was too much for her mother. There would
be no support there. In fact, Lee got the impression it
would be better if she just disappeared with her problem. Say, to Los Angeles.

Life had dealt a cruel blow to this bright eighteen-
year-old woman. It certainly didn't seem fair that so
many bad things should happen to her. She was mad,
and she let God know it. "Look, God, you could have
prevented this!" she yelled at him. "Why did you let
me open my stupid mouth at the office? Why did you
allow that man to invite me to his home? Why didn't
one of the other girls come, too? Do you realize I'm
too young for this responsibility? I never had a chance
to just be a kid. How come? Why couldn't I have enjoyed life for a while?"

Perhaps in that moment she was tempted to reject

her faith. She hadn't been a Christian for more than three months anyway. But who else could she turn to? He was the only One who seemed to care about her predicament. Venting her anger had helped.

She wasn't very familiar yet with the Bible, but she knew instinctively that this was where she needed to go for help. She flipped through its pages, not knowing where to look. Then she lost her grip and the Bible flopped open to Matthew:

> For if ye forgive men their trespasses, your heavenly Father will also forgive you: But if ye forgive not men their trespasses, neither will your Father forgive your trespasses (Matt. 6:14, 15).

Lee realized those words applied to her. If she was going to experience God's forgiveness, she had to forgive those who had hurt her. She thought of all the people who had hurt her over the years: her mother and father; teachers who had embarrassed her; friends who had rejected her; a boyfriend who had abruptly ended a relationship.

And her attacker.

Yes, the man who had disrupted her life and robbed her of her youth—how could she possibly forgive him? She didn't want to. Yet she had to. God had offered her a promise, *if* she'd obey.

As she hesitated, she thought of Jesus and how he had wrestled with God's plan on the night before he was crucified. Jesus understood what it was like to be a victim. He hadn't done anything wrong. But despite his personal emotions, he obeyed his Father.

Finally, she prayed, "Lord, I forgive him. I forgive him not because I feel like it, but because you have told me to do so."

Lee's life changed significantly that night. She had no husband, no mother, no father. She didn't even have a close friend. "Lord, you'll have to take their place," she prayed. "You be my husband, my father, my mother, my friend."

Lee's problem hadn't changed, but her perspective had changed radically. She was even able to view her future with a sense of adventure. Sure there were many uncertainties. But now she knew she wasn't traveling through this life alone.

Seven-and-a-half months later, on February 11, 1964, a healthy baby girl was born to Lee Kinney. Lee never saw her daughter. She'd arranged for the baby to be adopted. The only requirement she made of the county adoption agency was that the child be placed in a "Bible-believing home."

It wasn't easy to bury the memory of that child. Sometimes she consoled herself with the thought that she'd probably have children of her own someday. She often prayed for the baby, particularly that the child would come to know Christ.

The years passed and the memory of that bizarre episode faded. She was twenty-eight when she met a successful businessman—Hal Ezell—twice widowed, with two teenage daughters. They were married, and Lee legally adopted the daughters.

But Hal and Lee never had children of their own. As the teenagers grew and left home, Lee had to realize that the baby she'd had as a teenager would be her only one. But there was no pain in the realization. God had provided a rich life for her over the past twenty years. Yes, there was a piece missing, but she had learned to live without that piece because she had God's peace.

By now, Lee had learned much about the Bible. She had seen God do many good things in her life. Her gift for public speaking coupled with sensitivity for reaching out to hurting people, led her to teach women's groups and Bible studies. She wrote a book, called *The Cinderella Syndrome*. She even started a radio program: "Reflections." And her husband received a prestigious political appointment in President Reagan's administration.

It's a great story, but it doesn't end there. One day, shortly before Christmas 1984, Lee got a phone call. Lee's natural daughter had found her—after a three-year search!

Lee found it strange talking to a woman who was still a baby in her mind. Her daughter's name was Julie. She was married and had a baby, so Lee was now a grandmother.

They met for the first time two months later in Washington, D.C., where they celebrated Julie's twenty-first birthday.

Once Lee asked Julie why she had done the search. "Because I had to know if you had surrendered your life to Christ," Julie answered.

God had honored Lee's choice to trust him many years earlier. And how he had allowed her to see how he had taken a senseless tragedy and turned it into something beautiful.[9]

Jungle Madness 10

We hear about it on the news several times a year. A man goes berserk and murders his family; or shoots several people in the street; or systematically terrorizes a community with a series of murders. When his identity is revealed, often those most surprised are the neighbors. "He was so nice . . . kept to himself . . . the last person I'd imagine. . . ."

What made this person do it? Were there signs that might have warned us that he was psychotic? Could anyone have stopped him? We ask these questions for a day or two, then the story fades from our consciousness.

Perhaps a more sinister question we might ask of such a person is this: "Did he have a choice?"

This story is about a man who on the surface appeared to be a genuine minister of the gospel.

He was ordained and pastored a church in a respected mainline denomination.

He had a thriving, committed congregation.

The worship services were vibrant, full of emotion, bringing together people of diverse backgrounds— black and white, rich and poor, educated and illiterate.

A dedicated staff ministered with this man for years.

They were involved in an ongoing ministry of social action—feeding the poor, providing clothing and shelter for the disadvantaged, housing and caring for the aged and infirm, operating a drug-rehabilitation center.

People who were disenfranchised and in emotional need—the divorced, widowed, ex-prisoners, juvenile delinquents—found love and hope.

Civic leaders and entertainment celebrities lauded the work as a model of Christian charity.

But underneath the pious veneer, something was rotten. What appeared to be Christian really wasn't. And the deception would cause untold anguish and suffering.

The story begins in a small Indiana community. A devout church woman led a wayward boy into what appeared to be a sincere conversion. The boy was so inspired that he began carrying his Bible to school and preaching to his classmates. He visited most of the local churches, searching for a congregation that would give him the love he didn't experience in his broken home.

He felt most comfortable in a black Pentecostal church. He loved the gospel music and the warm, emotional style of worship. He determined then that Christians were missing out by segregating their services. Someday he would be a minister, and when he was, he would have an integrated church.

He began his formal ministerial career before he had even completed college. He was appointed pastor of a struggling congregation in a poor section of Indianapolis. He continued his studies while he plunged into his work. His first sermons were simple, pointing out moral lessons from the Bible. His style was warm, friendly, sincere. People were attracted.

The church in Indianapolis grew—partly because of the young preacher's charisma—partly because of the warm singing and open sharing—partly because of the dramatic prophecy and healing services—and partly because of the pastor's concern for social justice.

This minister didn't just talk about changing things; he modeled it. He and his wife adopted a black child and a Korean child. And they opened a free restaurant to provide meals for the needy.

But appearances can be deceiving. While hundreds of people packed the church services, there were others who weren't so sure about this young preacher. His closest boyhood friend was frightened by his domineering behavior. More than once he locked his friend in the barn. There were threats, and once he shot at his friend with a rifle while they were hunting. It wasn't an accident.

The minister's wife, Marci, wanted to leave him. Initially, she had been captivated by his charm and tenderness. He could always turn those on in a moment. But he also had a violent temper. He was jealously possessive. He smothered her so that she had no freedom. He constantly tested her loyalty. She had hoped for a partnership; he treated her like a slave. She might have left him except that she believed that marriage was for life. And she believed in her husband's ministry.

As a pastor, there were disturbing signs—a propensity for manipulation; a bizarre friendship with a cult leader named Father Divine; evidence that the "miracle" healings were only cleverly designed tricks; rambling sermons that could last several hours; church discipline that featured long interrogations and loyalty tests.

But most disturbing were his attacks against the Bible. He began to rail against the errors and contradictions he found in the Bible. The Book could not be trusted. Instead, he established himself as the authority over the lives of his congregation. He wanted to be called *Father*. When they prayed, they would pray to him.

Naturally, this didn't happen all at once. The changes came slowly. The outward appearance remained very Christian, very right.

But those who were closest to him saw more. Soon after his marriage, he stopped believing in God. From his observations, while working in a hospital and vis-

iting the poor, he decided that there was no God. A
merciful God could not possibly allow such suffering.
The church was not serving the needs of mankind.

He would change that. He did not enter the ministry because of a love for God but to aid the hurting—
and to somehow fulfill his craving for control over the
lives of people.

Sometime in his late teens or early twenties, a young
man chose to reject the God of the Bible. He rejected
the faith taught to him as a youth. He rejected the
authority of Scripture.

In God's place, he placed himself. He became his
own God. He—alone—would find the solutions for
man's sufferings.

While maintaining the outward trappings of Chris-
tianity, he sought to manipulate people into depen-
dence on him rather than God. He became the source
of love, encouragement, and discipline.

When a human being commits a despicable crime—
not a crime of passion, but one of cold-blooded mur-
der—it's not an instant decision. It's a process, built
step-by-step over many years. An entire thinking process must be constructed in order to rationalize the
act.

For Jim Jones the beginning of the end started with
a choice, as a teenager, to reject God. The downward
spiral began to accelerate when he moved his People's
Temple from Indianapolis to California. And it concluded in a jungle camp in British Guyana, on No-

vember 18, 1978, when he led nine hundred people to
their deaths in a mass-suicide ritual.

It's easy to say Jim Jones was a godless maniac. It's
even easier to say that we would never have been so
deceived. But the facts cause us to wonder.

Jones created an illusion of Christian respectability.
He knew how to toss around Christian jargon. He
preached that we must not just say we are Christians,
but we must show it with our actions.

In San Francisco the followers of Jim Jones were
very busy living out that message. They counseled the
jobless, operated a free health clinic, provided free legal aid to two hundred families per month, fed eight
hundred to eighteen hundred hungry per day.

His followers were not irreligious people. In fact,
almost everyone came from established churches. They
grew up in Christian homes, attended Sunday school,
memorized Bible verses, worshiped in church as
adults. Virtually every major denomination was
represented.

Could the tragedy of Jim Jones and the People's Temple be repeated? It can, and it has. It happens when
people look for their hope from a man—any human
being—instead of God.

It happens when Christian leaders forget their first
love and begin thinking of themselves more highly
than they ought.

It happens when people try to solve their own problems in their own efforts, rather than depending on
the ways of God.

It happens when Christians stop studying the Bible and asking the hard questions to determine what is of God and what is not.

Jim Jones was deceived when he chose to follow his ways rather than God. The tragedy of his life is that hundreds of others made a similar choice. They followed a man who claimed to be God and missed the message of the real God, revealed in Jesus Christ.

Their choice led to a jungle tragedy.[10]

The "Unclean" Doctor 11

For thousands of years, it's been considered a curse. Its victims are scarred for life—rejected by friends and loved ones—feared by the masses—unable to work—required to beg for their bread.

Slowly, their bodies deteriorate. Fingers and toes become useless stubs. Faces are disfigured. Sores fester and spread. They are alive but as though they were dead.

Their scourge is *leprosy*. One of the most dreaded diseases known to man. In Bible times, lepers were cast out of the community. If a healthy person inadvertently came too near them, they had to yell, "Unclean! Unclean!" They were society's social outcasts.

And so it remained for centuries. In 1950 there were

more than ten million victims of leprosy throughout the world. Some 2 million of them lived in India. The fortunate few lived in sanitariums. Most of the rest begged on the streets.

By then it was known by medical experts that there was only a very short period of time when leprosy was contagious. And there was no danger of contracting the disease from casual contact. Yet victims of the disease were outcasts.

What could one person possibly do about such a problem? It seemed so hopeless. With so many other needs in the world, why worry about one for which there was no cure? Why fight generations of prejudice against these people?

Yet Jesus Christ found lepers important in his ministry. He even reached out and *touched* these untouchables—and they were healed.

If Jesus found these outcasts important, worth saving, then surely we should, too. So thought one man, Dr. Paul Brand. He wanted to do something to help India's lepers. And he did. Because of an amazing secret he learned about the disease, he was able to change the thinking of medical experts around the world. Even more important, his discoveries gave hope and life to those who'd known neither.

It all began when Paul was a young missionary doctor at a medical college in Vellore, India. He was a very busy man. Hundreds of patients poured through the hospital every day. He taught a class in surgery. As one of only two surgeons on the staff, he faced problems that would challenge a physician with many more years of experience. On top of that, he was trying to learn the local Tamil dialect to better communicate with his patients.

Certainly, this man was doing plenty for the Lord. Why take on more responsibility? Especially in an area where others said nothing more could be done?

That was the choice Paul faced when he visited a leprosarium. Like most people, he had a mental image of those with leprosy. He knew that the fear of contracting the disease was unfounded, yet, he had to fight his natural tendency to feel repugnance as he strolled among the patients.

Gradually his professional curiosity got the better of him. Dr. Bob Cochrane, a dermatologist and the leprosarium's director, gave Paul various observations about the patients' skin as he conducted the tour. But Paul found his attention focusing on their *hands*.

As a surgeon, Dr. Brand was in awe of the intricate construction of the human hand. He considered the hand the most skillful and exquisite tool, with the exception of the brain, devised by God. Healthy hands, with years of training, might play a piano with the skill of Vladimir Horowitz, or paint a masterpiece like Leonardo da Vinci's "Last Supper," or handle a scalpel in the most delicate of operations.

The hands he saw at the leprosarium would never play an instrument or paint a canvas. Many of them looked more like claws than hands. The fingers, many of them nothing more than stubs, were stiff, inflexible—useless. Without healthy hands, how could these people ever hope to live productive lives?

Finally he asked his friend, "What's the matter with these hands? How do they get this way? What do you do about them?" Unfortunately, Dr. Cochrane could provide no answer.

Dr. Brand was shocked. How could Dr. Cochrane, a leprosy specialist, not know? Surely something could be done for these hands.

Dr. Cochrane immediately shot back a challenge. "I'm a skin man. But it's you, not I, who are the bone man, the orthopedic surgeon. I wonder if you can explain to me why, when there are more than ten million leprosy patients in the world, not one orthopedic surgeon has ever really studied the deformities of leprosy."

Dr. Brand could easily have agreed with his friend that someone should do something. Of all the surgeons in the world, surely one would feel the call to study this problem. But he, Paul Brand, already had more than one man could handle. Surely God didn't mean for him to accept this challenge?

The two men continued their stroll in silence. Paul saw a man trying to detach a leather strap from the buckle of his sandle, but it kept slipping out of his hands. Dr. Cochrane explained: "Nerve damage. There is absolutely no feeling after this type of leprosy has reached this particular stage, in either the hands or feet."

What a staggering realization. These hands would touch an object and feel nothing. In Tamil, he asked the leprosy victim if he could examine the man's hands. "Squeeze my hand," Paul requested. "Press as hard as you can."

Instantly, Paul felt intense pain shoot through his palm. The man's grip was like iron. No normal hand could have exhibited greater strength.

It was a moment that changed Dr. Brand's life. He realized that the man's hand, though seemingly crippled, was not paralyzed. There were still good muscles. Was there any way he could again make that hand useful?

At this point, Paul realized his divine call. This was why he was brought to India—to find an answer to those troubling questions. All he had to do was look into the faces of these victims to find compassion and motivation. Deep inside was a man or a woman, but they were reduced to the level of animals. Their minds had atrophied with their hands and feet, for what good was a brain when you couldn't even earn a day's meal? These people were condemned to a living hell. If only he could help them. . . .

Every spare moment now became devoted to his search for answers. He combed books and journal articles on reconstructive surgery and found no mention of leprosy. He begged the director of the medical school to let him use a few of the hospital's beds for leprosy patients. He wanted to experiment with some operations—on victims who had nothing to lose—and see if he could find some answers.

But victims of leprosy simply weren't allowed in

regular hospitals. Why take up valuable bed space
with patients who had no hope of recovery? They
would be a financial burden, for nearly all leprosy patients were penniless, unable to contribute anything
for their treatment. Plus they would frighten other
paying patients away.

Besides, everyone knew that these people had "bad
flesh." Could they even respond to normal surgical
procedures? What good would it do if their fingers
and toes were going to rot away and fall off?

It was that last question he had to address first. The
members of the hospital staff were not unsympathetic,
but they were skeptical. Dr. Brand first had to find out
if the concern about "bad flesh" was valid. For if it
was, then there was no use proceeding.

For several months the doctors and a band of helpers
visited leprosy sanitoriums within traveling distance
of Vellore. They examined and studied the histories of
nearly two thousand patients. Dr. Brand discovered
that paralysis occurred according to a strict pattern.
The muscles that were paralyzed were always the
same. The muscles that remained strong were also the
same. That meant he might surgically replace the paralyzed muscles with the healthy ones.

But that still didn't answer the question of rotting
appendages. The research continued. Assistants did
daily inspection of patient's hands, trying to catch the
moment when a finger was shortening. Paul studied
tiny specimens of skin and found there was no evidence of disease. In other words, the skin on their

hands was normal and healthy, except for the fact that they had no nerve endings. That meant the skin ought to heal normally.

That led to his first experiment in surgery. He had to smuggle his first patient into the hospital. He did tendon transplants on a man's thumb and fingers, followed by long periods of physical therapy. And it was a success. The patient's claw turned again into a human hand.

But that created a new dilemma. Once his patient was released, he returned to his life of begging. Because he still bore the scars of leprosy, no one would employ him. And because his hands were now healthy, fewer people took pity on him. The doctor realized he was creating beggars with less ability for begging. What these people needed was *a chance to earn a living*.

He established a small village where patients could live, learn a skill—in farming or carpentry—and become self-supporting. In time the medical school allowed construction of a new ward for leprosy patients, and Dr. Brand refined his surgical procedures. He also continued his research. He particularly was concerned about why patients lost fingers or toes. What was there in the disease that so cruelly removed part of their bodies?

The answer was the breakthrough that has changed our understanding of leprosy. Through his numerous patients and continual monitoring of them in their village as they learned to work, Dr. Brand discovered this truth. Without exception, there was a logical explanation, unrelated to the disease, for the damage to their fingers.

To explain, think for a moment about how your fingers tell you how much pressure you are exerting. Suppose you try to turn a stiff outdoor water faucet. When the metal begins to dig into your hand as you try to get a better grip, pain shoots a warning to your brain. As a result, you release the grip and look for a piece of cloth or a glove to protect your hand before trying again.

But suppose you felt no pain. Suppose you continued to exert force on the faucet, unaware that your skin was being cut and blood vessels were being opened. The normal daily tasks we take for granted often have devastating results for leprosy victims. We are warned by the presence of heat to keep our hands away from a hot stove. But they have no such warning and can suffer horrific burns.

Dr. Brand discovered that the victims of leprosy were not losing their fingers because of the disease. They were losing them because they couldn't feel the danger signals that we take for granted. However, if they could learn new habits—how to hold tools, how to adjust physical pressure, how to take precautions around dangerous equipment—they could preserve their hands indefinitely.

Now the doctor's surgery was for a purpose. He could restore a patient's hands, hence that person's ability to work. With that change, people were revived in their spirits. They became productive human beings again.

All of this was done in the name of Christ. There was no pressure exerted to make these people become Christians, but they saw the love of Christ in action. Often that was all they needed, and many became Christians.

Today, Dr. Brand leaves a legacy, born out of compassion for an oppressed group of people. As Christ reached out and touched the untouchables and restored them to life, so one man took a risk and reached out to India's 2 million lepers. As a result, many of them today have new life—physically and spiritually. And the knowledge and techniques Dr. Brand discovered have forever changed our perceptions of this once-dreaded disease.[11]

Looking for Love in All the Right Places 12

When does one know she's found Mr. Right? On what basis does one decide to marry? Or not to marry?

And what about God's will in this area? Will God really direct our choice of mate if we allow him? If so, how will he reveal this great news?

Those are good questions to ask now, whether or not you are contemplating marriage. Unfortunately, most people never think about what they require in a spouse until faced with the big question—*if then*.

You only need to review the latest divorce statistics to know how many tragic decisions are made in the name of love. But just how does one know she's found the right man? Dottie Youd faced such a moment, and nearly made the wrong choice.

In most respects, Dottie seemed well equipped to evaluate potential mates. She came from a strong family that instilled in her strong moral and ethical values. She was not about to be sucked into a premature, physical relationship. While such a foundation is ideal, that alone isn't enough to build a successful marriage.

A brief look at Dottie's life after high school graduation may reveal one process for making the right decision about who to marry.

Like most young women today, Dottie was encouraged to pursue a career. But the example of her parents made family an equally attractive alternative. "My Mom was one hundred percent mom," she says. "She never worked outside the home. She made a point of always telling me and my younger brother and sister what a privilege it was to be a parent." So Dottie's ultimate desire was to marry and be a mother.

Until that time, Dottie had some idealistic goals. She majored in sociology at college. She thought this course of study would give her a firm grasp of what was wrong with society, and provide some positive answers to help fix it. But the more she advanced in her studies, the more discouraged she became. Her professors thoroughly detailed the problems of society, but could provide no practical solutions.

Dottie also minored in philosophy, which further confused her. The courses exchanged the faith she'd learned as a youth in church for a confusing set of opinions. Sometimes, she thought, "if only there was a book written that explained reality—who God was and what was truth. I would follow my life by that book." Unfortunately, the great thinkers of history had such differing opinions, she concluded that there was no such book.

By her senior year, Dottie wasn't sure where her life was heading. Sociology and philosophy obviously weren't tickets to any lucrative career. Perhaps, she thought, she'd become a flight attendant.

It was in that context that she reluctantly accepted an invitation from a sorority sister to a meeting of Christians. There she saw a number of fellow students praying to a God who obviously was very real to them.

It was a staggering experience—so different from the churches she'd attended as a child. It was a contradiction of what the philosophers taught. This was the answer sociologists couldn't provide. Dottie wanted to know this God.

With her friend's help, Dottie entered into a personal relationship with God through Jesus Christ.

What's this got to do with marriage and the choice of a spouse? you ask. Hold on! We're getting there.

Of course, school wasn't all studies. There was an active social life. When Dottie dated, she naturally thought about the man she'd marry. She knew what she wanted—a guy who was like her father. A man who was sensitive, caring, loving, supportive. Certainly that wasn't asking too much.

While Dottie was a person with strong moral values, she wasn't sure *why* she held them. That changed as a Christian. As she began to study the Bible, she learned that God instructed men and women to enjoy sex—within the confines of marriage. And he did that so we could enjoy it to the fullest—without all the negative effects of immorality.

She also realized how important it was that her future husband have the same personal relationship with Christ. She wanted Christ to be at the center of her marriage. That would be the glue that cemented their relationship. Quite simply, she wanted to marry a radical for Christ, so she stopped dating guys who weren't Christians.

After graduation Dottie entered into Christian work. She went through special training, raised financial support, and reported for ministry on a college campus. She would help other students as her sorority sister had helped her.

On that campus was another staff member. He, too, was committed to Christ. They dated—had a lot of good times—shared similar convictions—enjoyed the same friends. Both passionately wanted to see the world reached for Christ. Naturally he asked for Dottie's hand in marriage.

It sounds so nice. So right. Oh, she knew it wasn't a perfect match, but then, was that really possible? The two of them had vastly different personalities; yet even that was intriguing.

So why was Dottie uncomfortable with this prospect? She couldn't say, but something was wrong.

What Dottie wanted was to know God's will. She read in Proverbs that she could search for wisdom, call out for insight, and cry aloud for understanding. "If you look for it as for silver and search for it as for hidden treasure," she read, "then you will understand the fear of the Lord and find the knowledge of God" (Prov. 2:4 NIV).

How she wanted that knowledge. Would God really reveal his will? Would he show her how to answer this man? Would he reveal why she felt such a tug-of-war in her heart? Alone, she fell on her knees and prayed.

As she prayed, Dottie realized that she cared deeply about this man. He was a good person. They shared many common interests. *But she did not love him.* There was no spark. No sirens. No tingling excitement. She could not marry him.

With that resolved, she felt God's peace. The promised treasure—it was the wisdom and confidence to say no.

The young man was very gracious and understanding as Dottie explained her decision. Soon he left for another ministry assignment, easing any tension they might have felt. But there was also an emptiness. Dottie began to wonder if she'd have another chance. After all, everything seemed so right—except for one element. *Why couldn't that element have been there?*

Still there were no regrets. Dottie knew she had done the right thing. God had given her the confidence to make the right decision.

Some girls might say it's better not to marry than to marry the wrong person. They're right, but Dottie doesn't make that statement casually. She adds that it would be far better to be single forever than to be locked in a wrong relationship. As a Christian she knew she could wait.

A year later, Dottie again received a proposal for marriage. This time, the situation was different in one important way. With this man she had the emotions of love—plus everything else! All the good elements she'd had with the other guy were there—in greater magnitude.

And yet, she wondered. When this man popped the question, she honestly answered, "If you want me to give you an emotional answer, I'll say yes right now." But, she added, so many people marry because they're madly in love—yet look at the divorce rate. Certainly emotions alone don't make a good marriage. How could she know for sure that *this man* was God's will? God wasn't going to drop a note to her from the clouds, or speak to her audibly.

This potential husband was spiritually discerning. He suggested that Dottie take a piece of paper and draw a line down the middle. Then, in an attitude of prayer, on one side she should write down why she should marry him. On the other side, she would write all the reasons why she should not marry him. Perhaps then the answer would become clear.

Dottie did that early the next morning. She listed all the positives—how this man had the approval of her parents, how they shared similar goals, and how she liked his philosophy of parenting. And most important—that she loved him.

There were no items on the opposite side. She couldn't think of one reason not to marry this man!

Now that's about as close as most of us will come to having a divine note fall from the clouds. "It couldn't be any clearer," Dottie says. "Once I realized that everything was in place, I was free to say *yes!* And say it with conviction."

And who was this prince of a man? His name is Josh McDowell—popular speaker on college campuses and renowned author of more than twenty-two books. He's also mastermind of the "Why Wait" campaign, encouraging teenagers to wait until marriage for sex. And he's the proud father of Dottie's four children.

Most certainly, Dottie is glad she waited: "If I'd gone on my own emotion, or lack of it, life would be different now. If I had not obeyed God, then I could have gone my own way. Maybe some of the situations would have turned out fair. But they certainly wouldn't have been exciting like my life is now. I would have missed out on an incredible man for my life!"[12]

Epilogue:
A Fork in the Road

Have you given any thought to the ministry? I mean full-time service for the Lord, as a pastor, or missionary, or doctor, or teacher, or evangelist? Some graduates have, and are preparing to go to Bible college or seminary. But many have other plans, and full-time Christian work isn't part of those plans. Okay, no problem. But you need to be warned: God may have a different idea.

Alfred Guthrie had one great desire in life, and it wasn't serving God. Little did he realize that his interest would someday take him into the ministry.

His love was sports. Like many young boys, he dreamed of playing major league baseball. However, he had one small problem. His athletic ability just didn't match his desire. That was a fact he had to acknowledge one evening when he achieved his crowning moment in high school sports.

You see Alfred was twelfth man on the junior-varsity basketball team. And that team won only one game all season. And lost twenty-one. Still, history can't deny him his place in the record book.

The team was playing it's archrival, and as usual, losing—badly. With two minutes to play in the first half, they were behind 34-4. So the coach inserted our hero. Alfred proceeded to wear down the opposition by committing four fouls in one minute and twenty seconds before the coach yanked him. That's a school record that still stands twenty-four years later.

Well, if Alfred couldn't compete on the field, then he'd find another way to participate. So he put to use two of his genuine talents—writing and math. He became official scorekeeper and statistician for the varsity teams. He was sports editor of the school paper. He wrote for the town weekly. And he was good enough as a writer to win a state-wide journalism contest in the sports-writing division.

So what's all that got to do with ministry? Well, nothing—yet. Alfred thought about his future. When he graduated from high school, his plan was to go to college, major in math, and prepare to become a high school teacher. Oh, he also arranged to use his writing and statistical skills. He helped pay his way through school by working for his college's sports-information department.

The plan was sound but it had one flaw. When Alfred reached his senior year, there were too many teachers and not enough jobs. Besides that, Uncle Sam was indicating he might want Alfred's services. The Vietnam War was raging, and eligible young men faced a draft lottery. Now what would he do?

He could try prayer. Some fraternity brothers encouraged him to revitalize a relationship he'd begun with Christ in the fifth grade. After attending a retreat, he prayed a simple prayer: "God, I've tried running my own life, and I've reached a dead end. I give myself totally to you. I'm ready to let you run my life." In that moment, he realized the security he could have, even when his future was uncertain.

Alfred was on the right track, but he had a few things to learn about how God directs a life. When the draft lottery didn't call his name, Alfred decided to give God two years of his time. His plan was to go and be an evangelist on a college campus. Then he'd check the job market again to see if he could get a teaching position.

The organization he joined had a publications department, and they heard about Alfred's writing experience. They asked him to consider editing a magazine about Christian athletes. And would he give them his decision the next morning?

What was God trying to tell him? He'd never even considered that his writing skills could be used in ministry. Late that night, he sat alone under a palm tree and decided he would not go to bed until God revealed his will. But how does one hear God speak in a situation like that? Alfred didn't know, but he was determined to find out.

As he prayed, Alfred opened his Bible. He felt impressed to look in the concordance. Under the word *ability* he saw four listings. Two were in the Old Testament. One was about how people gave money according to their ability for the rebuilding of God's temple. The other told about the special abilities of several young men to serve in the king's palace.

In the New Testament, Alfred read: "And unto one he gave five talents, to another two, and to another one; to every man according to his ability" (Matt. 25:15, Scofield). This, of course, was the start of the parable of the talents. Apparently Christ was saying that some people had more ability, and therefore more responsibility to use what had been given to them. He praised those who invested their talents, and condemned the servant who buried his talent in the ground.

Then he read the other verse: ". . . if any man minister, let him do it as of the ability which God giveth: that God in all things may be glorified through Jesus Christ . . ." (1 Peter 4:11).

Alfred shut his Bible and thanked God for the answer. Clearly, God seemed to be directing him into writing. If God had given him the ability to write, and wanted to use that ability for his kingdom, then Alfred was willing to try it.

Seventeen years later, Alfred still has not made it to the classroom. His plans changed because he allowed

God to direct his path. It didn't seem completely logical at the time. After all, in college he'd majored in math, not English or journalism. Surely he should have prepared more for this career. He says today that he got four years of college journalism in six months of on-the-job training.

God's path led Alfred to edit and write for several magazines. Then he started writing books. All of his writing was for the purpose of bringing people to a fuller understanding of God through Jesus Christ. Without intending to do so, he had wound up in ministry. It wasn't preaching or missions, and he hadn't gone to seminary—but his writing was changing lives. God was using his abilities to lead people to Jesus Christ. His stories about Christian athletes were motivating young people to live totally for Christ, just as he had learned to do himself. His collaborations with various Christian leaders were enabling more people to benefit from their Bible teaching.

So far, Alfred has written twenty books. And this is one of them. For Alfred Guthrie is Alfred (Al) Guthrie Janssen, the author of the book you've just read.

It is my prayer that you have found these stories inspiring, and that you have seen in a fresh way the many ways God can work in and through your life.

Source Notes

I am grateful for these materials and interviews that I relied on for certain chapters of the book.

1. "To Fear God or Man" George Reed with Dave Hunt, *Fear No Man* (Eugene, Ore.: Harvest House, 1987).

2. "Learning from Failure" Madeleine L'Engle, *A Wrinkle in Time* (1962), *A Circle of Quiet* (1972) (N.Y.: Farrar, Straus & Giroux), pp. 21-22, 139-40; *Walking on Water* (Marissa, Ill.: Shaw, 1980), p. 60; plus an interview with Madeleine L'Engle.

3. "A Modern Philosopher" Russell Miller, *The Real Story of Playboy* (N.Y.: Holt, Rinehart & Winston, 1984), plus several magazine articles.

4. "Coaching on a Higher Level" "One More Season," a PBS documentary, and several newspaper and magazine articles, plus an interview with Charles and Lucy Wedemeyer.

5. "Caught in the Conflict" Leilani Watt with Al Janssen, *Caught*

in the Conflict: My Life with James Watt (Eugene, Ore.: Harvest House, 1984).

6. "Who Said Life Was Fair?" Based on an interview with Butch Carter in 1986.

7. "Good Grades or More Fun?" Steve Douglass with Al Janssen, *How to Get Better Grades and Have More Fun* (San Bernardino, Calif.: Here's Life Publishers, 1985).

8. "Searching for Freedom" Robin Lee Graham, *Dove* (N.Y.: Harper & Row, 1972) and Robin Lee Graham and Derek Gill, *Home Is the Sailor* (N.Y.: Harper & Row, 1983).

9. "Aftermath of Terror" Lee Ezell, *The Missing Piece* (Eugene, Ore.: Harvest House Publishers, 1986).

10. "Jungle Madness" Tim Reiterman with John Jacobs, *Raven: The Untold Story of the Reverend Jim Jones and His People* (N.Y.: E. P. Dutton, 1982); Mel White, *Deceived!* (Old Tappan, N.J.: Spire Books, (Revell, 1979); James Reston, Jr., *Our Father Who Art in Hell: The Life and Death of Jim Jones* (N.Y.: Times Books, 1981).

11. "The 'Unclean' Doctor" Dorothy Clarke Wilson, *Ten Fingers for God* (N.Y.: McGraw Hill, 1965); Dr. Paul Brand and Philip Yancey, *Fearfully & Wonderfully Made* and *In His Image* (Grand Rapids: Zondervan, 1980, 1984).

12. "Looking for Love in All the Right Places" is based on an interview with Dottie McDowell in 1988.